AF584232
Photo by J Taki

Sydney is on Gadigal land, the traditional land of the Gadigal people, the original inhabitants. The Gadigal are part of the Eora Nation, a group of coastal Aboriginal people. We wish to acknowledge them and thank them for caring for this country.

Photo by Anderson Mendes

SHINING CITY SYDNEY

A TOUR THROUGH THE POET'S EYE

LIBBY HATHORN & ELIZABETH CUMMINGS

Photo by Elizabeth Cummings

Foreword

Since creating our collection of poems *Coastal; From Yarra Bay to Watson's Bay*, we have looked to our home city as a source. We hope that by capturing the familiar as well as some more secret parts of Sydney, both locals and intrepid tourists will enjoy a deeper insight into this shining city.

Elizabeth Cummings (EC)

Visitors to Sydney can easily find details of many famous tourist spots they might like to visit. We wanted to imbue a personal point of view about individual locations. With such a shining harbour at its heart it's not difficult to find places and people in Sydney that inspire.

Libby Hathorn (LH)

Poems

Into Sydney

Parks, Gardens, Water Views

Sydney Identities

Shining Places

Photo by Anderson Mendes

Into Sydney

Sydney Shining City

Sydney diamond city
of glittering waterways
harbours and beaches
shining city.

Diamond city
sapphire city
emerald city
hugged with rugged
coastal growth
tamed with parks
and interlacing streets
diamond hard
yet water enticing
presenting in all its jewels
a shining city
welcoming and open-hearted.

LH

The Wonderful World of Sydney

That feeling I've always known you Sydney,
great powerful emerald and sapphire city
embracing all your visitors and game players
who cruise into your harbour finding other common spaces.
Your resting places; chair or bench or under a mighty gum,
inviting all to feel free to kick off shoes,
lie back in the manicured grass
or wander arterial streets, discovering
many a gallery and museum.

Temptress city, you with myriad culinary delights
discovered in lane ways stuffed with choices,
early morning coffee spots, magical sticky pastries.
Late into the night, you offer bar stools
with lustrous lapping waterfronts
for all to sip the fanciest of cocktails
mix, mingle, meet
before chasing the last trams and taxis home
sending revelers tumbling into rainbow sheets
or hotel-grade, thread-count luxury linens,
as your Sydney siren song seduces.
Be free. Free to wander, free to wonder too!
You're welcome here.

EC

Flying with the Moon over Sydney

Tonight I took an evening flight
and through the window shone such bright
looking out was thrilled to see
a full moon gleam on a cloudy sea
on the wings all through the night
like a guide, a sign just right.
Kept peering out to check it there,
to marvel, wonder and to stare.
I travelled happy with this old moon
that seemed to say, "You'll be home soon!"

EC

Photo by Anderson Mendes

The Rocks

Some Walking Tours

From the thrumming hustling Circular Quay
Walk round the ocean foreshores
To step into the past...
The Rocks, the stalwart!
Cobbled roads and veering stairways
Craggy sandstone rocks
Grainy sandstone buildings...
The Rocks, the steadfast!

Tour the ancient Aboriginal tracks
Hear First Nation stories
(maybe a Welcome to Country)
Regard shorelines, and thrill to insight
Into precious Dreamtime stories.
The Rocks, the indefatigable!

Then tour
Colonial Sydney and stories of
Convicts made good or bad
Buildings of a checkered past
Swerving lane ways once bedraggled
Now bright with shops and tourist treats
Discover secret places
Nooks and crannies that abound,
And courtyards, corners, breezeways, parks,
Or just stay put, gaze across the harbour
To Bridge and Opera House and open sky!
Linger here...
The Rocks, the magnanimous!

LH

Photo by Anderson Mendes

Sydney Opera House

Monumental shells
House bespeaking
harbour
    sails
        birds' wings

A spherical geometry
14 shells a perfect sphere
Jon Utzon
    Danish architect
        genius

Rising, rising
Even amid discordance rising,
14 shells a perfect sphere

Sydney Opera House
Changed the image
    of a harbour
        of a city
            of a country.

This sculpted shape
A geometry that soars
Pitch perfect!

LH

Mother Ship

Sydney Opera House
our mighty mother ship
alien vessel
born of a foreign mind
commissioned by Cahill
in 1955, with a mission,
to house operatic performances
to be a beacon
communicate and connect
what it is to be human
human dreams, human failings
trauma and discord
resignation and conflict
love and human triumph.

Many have performed
an *Autopsy on this Dream*,
this craft on grand design,
this icon, this vantage point,
often a meme with billboard roof.
With feminine curves
nurturing and connecting the world
in diverse cultures, new ideas,
untold narratives and flourishing talent.
Let the show go on!

EC

Photo by Anderson Mendes

Sydney Harbour Bridge

A graceful arch
of brute strength steel.
Eight years to connect
steel halves meeting
19th August 1930
Dawes Point to Milsons
city to the north side,
north side to city side.

Now daring parties tied together
daily make the Bridge Climb
ascend to tourist views
a thrilling spectacle
of a shining city.
53,000 tons of steel
at least 8 million rivets
granite pylons hewn by
Scot and Italian settled at Moruya town
for years, to ply their artful trade.

Opening Ceremony
9th March 1932 upset
a figure on horseback
flying forward with sword
to slice the opening ribbon
his name De Groot
forever in our history.

Sydney and its bridge
aflame every New Year's Eve
announcing to the world
its place, a graceful arch
of brute strength steel.

LH

Circular Quay

Tally ho!
Alight at Circular Quay
set your sights dockside,
the skyscrapers, financial giants,
tourist meccas.
Dear Opera House
splendid span Harbour Bridge.
Destinations, destinations,
never more than a few steps
to another memorable view.
The old goal, the laneways, The Rocks,
the long booked-out restaurants
all offering memories.

Do you recall visions of New Year's Eve
cast to every sitting room as clocks struck 12?
Do you recall Cinderella moments,
spangling fireworks, rock star concerts,
the little tugs and water taxis
bouncing among ferries yellow and green?

Here, tourists and commuters colliding
in myriad fashions, diverse languages
and every one of them with phone in hand
be it for business or bucket lists
all on parade at Circular Quay.
Tally ho!

EC

Circular Quay Escapades

A focal point for divergence
A nub, a heart and soul of Sydney,
A hard-working merry ferry hub.

Go North to Manly of Fairy Bower fame
Or East to Watson's Bay with walks and fish'n'chips divine
Or West to Parramatta with its surprise of new and old
Or round to Barangaroo with walks and eats and views.

Circular Quay, ferries to lure
A nub, a heart and soul of Sydney,
A hard-working merry ferry hub.
What journeys and escapades!

LH

Photo by Dominic Kurniawan Suryaputra

by Anderson Mendes

Passenger Terminal Haiku

Colossal cruise ships
sail too big for the harbour
terminal misfits.

EC

Ferry Ride to Barangaroo

Bridge to the left, Opera House to the right
churning water till ferry-stop comes into sight.
Commuters keen spill off and on
thrum of the engine in winter sun.

Winding paths and changing faces
parks and ledges resting places,
look-out spots to bide your time
cafes and restaurants, a fulsome line,
bustle of city high-rise nearby
but here at the dock there's an arc so high!
Barangaroo all water and sky!

LH

Luna Park Harbourside

There it is the famous face
fierce toothy smile
red, red lips, dark staring eyes
and a spikey rising sun crown!
Walk through the clown's mouth
engulfed at once
fantasy art deco architecture.

Through a volatile history
from 1935 through several sad closures,
its vantage point on harbour's edge
spelling redevelopment and high rise,
rallies saved the park,
artists saved the grinning face.

The Luna Park Reserve Trust
made it safe with fresh new rides.
Hair-raisers still,
dippers, flingers, Ferris wheels
and the only surviving
wild mouse ride in the world.
Luna Park harbourside
bold open-mouthed face
keeps smiling and ingesting thrill-seekers,
earning its hard-won place
in an exhilarating harbourscape.

LH

Coca-Cola
FRIENDSHIP
SYDNEY

Photo by Anderson Mendes

Marrinawi Cove at Barangaroo

Barangaroo to the Harbour Bridge
a new promenade a-top walls
Marrinawi Cove
scootering children helmet-clad
ambling adults, lunchtime sprinters,
zippy council carts, here in their own world.

Marrinawi Cove revived
living and breathing.
with swimming and fishing,
the newness of solar capsule lights
and neon runners' compression socks
round a cleaner bay within the harbour
a new page of history.

EC

I Love the Trams

Those sliding, sloping, sleek red snakes,
I love the trams, the time it takes
to watch them glide across the road,
indifferent to their people load,
blunt-nosed slinky urban snakes
powerful too, no time it takes,
to gather speed and whoosh along
a whirring, gentle humming song.

Not like the trams, the toast-rack wide,
the ones in childhood we would ride,
noisy on their gnashing tracks,
swaying riders from front to back.
Clanging bells and paperboys,
a screechy, rattly, pleasing noise,
gather speed and whoosh along
air alive with their raucous song.

LH

The Tramsheds at Forest Lodge

Trams, iron clad beauties
Saved; an Inner West playground
For all to enjoy.

EC & LH

Photo by Elizabeth Cummings

Parks, Gardens,
Water Views

Centennial Park in Stages

1811 the birth of a park
490 acres of Sydney Commons
1824
new water sources
1866
Sydney Common Improvement Act
for sport and active recreation
included Moore Park.

26th January 1888
the park's official opening
the fruition
of Sir Henry Parkes plans
a People's Park.

A park! A park!
for the people
to breathe and thrive.
A park! A park!
for the people
378 acres wide.
A park! A park!
once Kangaroo Ground.
A park! A park!
Centennial Park
the People's Park is found.

EC

Centennial Park

Nature Positive 100 times

100 trees, 100 garden beds,
100 people, prams, pushers, bikers,
strollers, sitters, picnickers,
walkers, gazers, thinkers.
100 bushes, branches, breathing spaces,
Green Jewel Park in suburbia.

100 swamps and ponds,
reeds that praise them,
eels that deep frequent,
ducks that go on top,
with water lilies spread.

Green Jewel Park in suburbia
And in evening light 100,000
bats take flight!

In the name a hundred,
a hundred times a gift,
Centennial Green a gift,
nature positive here,
Green Jewel Park in suburbia,
ever nature positive.

LH

Photos by Anderson Mendes

Photo by Botanical Gardens of Sydney

Royal Botanical Gardens

Corpse Flower Blooming

Last week it was reported 'Putricia' the Corpse Flower
had 20,000 visitors lining up for hours to see her.
Crinkly skirt, velvety crimson, fluted leaves
sheath-like spike, its creamy green point
growing upwards it seems before one's eyes
in this glass hothouse with steam swirling.
The smell intensifies and gardeners on phones
give minute by minute reports on Putricia,
'She's just about ready' – (gasps) 'well about 20 minutes
and we can pollinate!'

A delicate operation
hand-pollinating the precious cache within,
live-streaming keeping the world informed.
(Some even wept when they saw her begin to open.)

She raises her body temperature tempting insects
and staff, who hover anxious and grateful to view
Amorphophallus titanium this 'giant deformed penis.'

This inflorescence is the first time in 15 years
Putricia has chosen to splay herself, just 24 hours,
staging her bold bloom, and offering her putrid smell
cadaver like, dead possum like, wet socks like,
before she collapses in on herself and dies,
staff at the ready to pollinate by hand
and gather her fertile seeds for the world
as her numbers dwindle dangerously.
So many other botanical treasures bypassed
just to say 'I saw Putricia.'

At least 20,000 were here to see...

LH

Photo by Botanical Gardens of Sydney

A Date on Cockatoo Island

A short ferry ride from Circular Quay
Cockatoo Island surrounded by sea and city horizons.
Visitors of old may not have felt so lucky
housed in this infamous convict site.
Still rich in history, set for an event.
be it pop, opera, or camping.
Site for Sydney's biennale art.

Daring campers enjoy a strange night
with flickers of lights from the city aplenty;
cautious tours through austere buildings
eerie walks through mysterious tunnels
then in the inky night lie listening
for roaming fellow campers
and last tooting ferries.
Beware this nightlong adventure,
A convict history, 1839 to 1869.
Ghastly, ghostly tales could disturb sleep!

Come the morning, the sparkle of sun
the smell of coffee, the chatter and clatter
of fresh gleeful tourists; oblivious
to what magic lies await.

EC

Taronga Zoo

Harbourside. Breezy ferry ride,
setting out on bushy paths or sky-high rides
soon to see those wonder animals inside
Taronga!
Amphibians and reptiles
frilled lizard or eyelash viper,
African Savannah tour
mud baths for baby hippos
meercats and zebras
alongside the waterholes,
tiger elephant gorilla.
Birds in flight amazing
galahs and cockatoos and eagles.
Giraffes and babies
in their tall enclosure
pandas and their babies too.
All the while harbourside
backdrops this zoo of wonder.
Taronga!

Walking and cavorting
racing and pacing
sniffing and snuffling
nuzzling and guzzling
teasing and pleasing
pouncing and pounding
animal lore, enclosures galore
staring and glaring
skimming and winning
flying and diving
wallowing and wonderful.
Wondrous animals!
Taronga!

LH

Photo by Jack McCracken

Paddington Reservoir Gardens

Grassy knolls under verdant canopy
arches for Sydney's historic water systems
vantage points to times gone by
now a public space; an outdoor room;
A peaceful break area for picnics and shade.
Back up on the street, crowds mill,
flow, and ebb on busy pavements
seeping in and out of shops,
restaurants, and pubs.
A human stream; a living waterway.
Garden harmony opposite commercial bustle.
Contrasting, complementary, communal.

EC

Photo by Shutterstock

Nutcote House

We were all once children and some of us lucky to know
"The Complete Adventures of Snugglepot and Cuddlepie."
May Gibbs their creator, much loved by kids so long ago.
This stalwart of Australian children's literature
used to live and write here at Nutcote House.
Designed by another national favourite;
architect; B.J. Waterhouse.
This harbourside cottage is now open to all,
May's life and work, guaranteed enchantment
in the whimsical gardens where her plant name puns
inspire today's custodians of her place to curate,
and like May Gibbs, find their best ideas
in nature out in the gardens of Nutcote.

EC

At Nutcote, North Sydney

Nutcote museum, home of May Gibbs (1877–1969),
a famous Australian children's illustrator and author.

Mother of the Gumnuts
May Gibbs, whose bush creatures
Snugglepot and Cuddlepie intrigue
many a child,
whose fiercesome Big Bad Banksia
equally terrify and delight!

Nutcote, her museum house,
with many a Scotty dog in her garden,
Nutcote, a breezy ferry ride on the harbour
welcomes you with the redolence of a rich past
and with an enchantment, this singular woman's
art and life.

LH

Photo by Elizabeth Cummings

Lunchtime in Hyde Park

Lunchtime sees city workers
all running gym-clad
over geometric slashes of pathways.
Canvas blobs of colour in their vests and visors
whilst annual blooms festoon garden beds
making garlands around the splendid central fountain
where marble man and boar cavort in rude nudity.

Tree lined avenues in dappled light
make ceremonial pathways
to Hyde Park's Anzac Memorial.
Luminous Art Deco monument mirrored
in the Pool of Reflection
for lunchtime strollers.

EC

Wendy Whiteley's Neverland

Do you believe in fairies?

Wendy's belief, her vision to create
beauty from the dumping ground
a Neverland if you will.
A landscape crafted with fertile palette
green hues, beside water colours
of lovely Lavender Bay.

Why can't you stay like this forever?

Through the years battles raged
over the existence of this guerrilla garden
with its new purpose, new life.
So, join in the fairytale magic
found here now and if you like,
believe!

EC

Wendy's Garden Haiku

Bush turkeys, plants, trees
Forged fitted for new design
Constant stream of folk.

EC

Wendy Whiteley's Secret Garden

Stone stairs plunge, broaden, encircle
then plunge again ever towards the harbour.
Wendy's garden, not so secret,
delays explorers, tempts them
to sit and talk and view garden and harbour.
Thick trees. Umbrella branches dark leaves
root us to nature talk, then perhaps
those bits and piece that may bedevil us,
personal exchanges. But easier out here
not to talk at all. Taking in stone stages,
wooden seats, slashes of harbour
performing through the ancient figs.

Behind, the house's quirky tower and
a plaque denoting a famous painter
once lived here, Brett Whiteley,
borrowing and rendering these views.
And in her garden, his partner Wendy
becomes a painter of another sort.

LH

Photo by Elizabeth Cummings

Running Past
Mrs Macquarie's Chair

Dear Mrs Macquarie,
I'm thinking of you
reposing on your chair
carved by convicts
at Yurong Point
with its vantage to naval fleet
and leisure vessels.
No doubt your pensive rest
nowadays would be disturbed
by runners in their masses
coursing around
the outcrop you have made your home
claiming it as your own
as we runners do today.
And your husband, the esteemed
Governor Lachlan Macquarie,
urbanist, planner and emancipist
yet still humanly capable of revenge
against those native to the land,
what do you make of his beliefs?

Mrs Macquarie,
if you were here today
would you still sit
and gaze out at portside ships
or would you be tempted
to descend your rocky pew
to join us on our run?

EC

Photo by Elizabeth Cummings

Photo by Anderson Mendes

Shop

Bondi Beach Haiku I

Utmost sea, sand, sky,
hard not to be amazed,
again, and again.

LH

Bondi Beach Haiku II

Bodies in the surf,
sun-languid watchers, only
dream of riding waves.

LH

Photo by Elizabeth Cummings

Bondi Beach Supreme

The dip, the plunge, the shock, the dream.
Timeless exuberance, Bondi Beach supreme.
Your moods flow as ours,
as the push and pull of tides.
Faces to the wind,
waves to the beach
horizon to vast sky
ours for the looking.
The bathers, the surfers, the board riders,
the watchers, the listeners, the learners,
the mishmash of the sun adoring
strewn across pale sand.

The dip, the plunge, the shock, the dream.
Timeless exuberance, Bondi Beach supreme.

LH

Photo by Anderson Mendes

Sydney's Coastal Surprises

Bondi to Coogee Walk

Underwater treasure
heaving rocks upon rocks
half-dragged out of the water
like some gin soaked half-drowned
drunken sailor sprawled motionless.
Left at the mercy of lapping waves
until moon, tide, with seasons collide
in a terrestrial alignment
and out of the depths rises
Mackenzie's Beach.

EC

Mackenzie's Haiku

Azure lace-white sea
Mythical Mackenzie's Beach
Once in seven years.

EC

Photo by Dillon Hunt

At Manly

At Manly you can
Surf, snorkel, swim,
Walk, wander, wonder!

Manly Beach
Regard a sunny seemingly endless
curling coastline
fringed with considerable pines
dark, admirable seaside trees.

Fairy Bower
Take an oceanside walk from
this splendid beach leading
to a shining place, a bower
and serene retreat
with jetty and bushland.

And Manly himself?
Wonder about this name.
A muscular Aboriginal man?
Or more, a healthy people
whose stature and wellbeing
1788, early inspired such a name?
Ahh! the Gayemagal people
traditional custodians of this land.

LH

Photo by Elizabeth Cummings

Beside You

Right here in this cemetery
a history of Sydney identities revealed; -
Cricketer and poet, politician and peer.
And many a citizen unknown,
Alongside tragic graves of children
Earning angels and crosses.
I might take the pleasure of a graveside ramble.
On tourist tracks with maps,

Or be a solitary wanderer free to dream
Melancholy dreams.

LH

Dorothea and Henry

Dorothea Mackellar. Henry Lawson.
On this cemetery trail
past poets inspire with old fashioned names
but with words and lines still resonating
"I love a sunburnt country ..." Dorothea
"I'm the Mother bush who bore you," Henry
Timeless ...

LH

Standing in Waverley Cemetery

A compendium of people and emotions

Sandstone gully
ocean lapping down below
between heavens and the deep
top heavy with marble headstones
history laden.
Gazing upon these names and places
these sinking, forgotten, crumbling graves.

I wonder about their residents...
A wave crashes,
drawing my eyes
towards the skyline
beyond which home, my first home,
and other marvelous lands lie hidden.

My history, my dreams stirring.
Cruise and cargo ships drift,
tiny on the horizon.
Parallel lives continuing.

EC

Photo by Elizabeth Cummings

Photo by Elizabeth Cummings

Sydney Identities

GRAFFITO ETERNITY

Arthur Stace 1885-1967 Sydney identity known for scribing the word Eternity for over 35 years on pavements and walls.

'Without beginning or end'
but there was his beginning in dire poverty,
his life tattered by War and Depression
Arthur, soldier, petty criminal, alcoholic
grog runner to brothels and two-up schools.
Then his call from God to shout Eternity.
Eternity
in the streets of Sydney
Eternity
on the streets of Sydney.

Arthur, weeping in the park
under a fig tree
after a sermon by Rev Hammond
at a Men's Meeting for 300
reformed alcoholics,
cup of tea and a rock cake
and the gift of the abiding word
Eternity
6 bob a day to keep him
scribing his way through days
through life
with chalk on pavements and walls
in an elegant hand
Eternity

At the turn of millennium
some 33 years after his death
and after 20 blazing minutes,
fireworks spectacular
as the smoke settled
emblazoned on the Sydney Harbour Bridge
for all the world to see
in his perfect copperplate handwriting
Graffito ETERNITY.

Sydney honoured this soul
Arthur Malcolm Stace
lost and found.

LH

Eternity

Photo State Library of NSW

B MILES
'MUST GIVE US PAUSE'

To be or not to ...

An eccentric who travelled on Sydney buses and trams and quoted Shakespeare for payment.

The wide blue bus that trundled us home
taking suburban corners to Tamarama Beach
with such a swing and such a roar
all the valley knew we'd arrived.
One day perched at the back
on the famously throw-about seat
the famous Sydney identity
our mothers called with sympathy
poor old Bea Miles, the vagrant.

A large lady of dark navy dress
sun visor perched
and big buttoned men's raincoat
bag slung across a big shoulder
bright eyes, eager hands
pointing to her sign
I quote Shakespeare.
Any speech on request.

We were schoolgirls
amused, afraid, but she descended
and we succumbed fetching coins from pockets
and pressing them into an eager hand.
Ahh Hamlet then, please...

To be or not to be that is the question
whether tis nobler in the mind to suffer
the slings and arrow of outrageous fortune
or take arms against a sea of troubles
and by opposing, end them.

Our mothers told us Bea
came of a good north shore family,
(never knowing of her father's violence).
Clever erratic, to university for a time
in a mental hospital for a time,
in goal for shorter times too.
Pinned a 5 pound note to her dress
so as to avoid arrest but still
a vagrant, who slept in church doorways,
and a cave for a time,
money from her family time to time,
took taxis ridiculous distances
once to Perth and paid the whole fare.
No home, no religion. The Little Sisters of the Poor
took her in and a kindly taxi driver,
hither and thither still to recite
those poems to passersby.

To die, to sleep...
To sleep perchance to dream: ay, there's the rub
for in that sleep of death what dreams may come
when we have shuffled off this mortal coil,
must give us pause.

LH

CINDRIC'S TROLLEY

Joseph Cindric, a migrant to Sydney in 1948, pushed his trolley for many years round the streets of Sydney. A replica of his homemade trolley can be found in the Powerhouse Museum.

Pushing his dreams,
man-machine one,
his memories are secret,
his hoard is hard won.

Pushing his life
the trolley stash grows,
A son, wife, a lover,
his letters, who knows?

What's Cindric's story
a migrant who's come
to live a new life here?
Yet something's undone.

Pushing his dreams
things never fulfilled,
faces swim round him,
sweet and young still?

He's rumpled and dirty
a man gone adrift
yet deep in the trolley
among things spin drift,
he carries a story
knows it's his to keep,
parades it through Sydney,
yet buries it deep.

Pushing his life,
man-machine one,
Cindric's memories are
secret,
his hoard is hard won.

LH

EDGECLIFF ANGEL 1

Simple strokes
a graceful dance across the walls and bridges
the Edgecliff Angel
perennial muse
hastily painted
illegally commissioned
pirouettes as we walk by.
This Edgecliff Angel
dancer unknown
painted so lovingly
was theirs an affair?

EC

Photo by Elizabeth Cummings

EDGECLIFF ANGEL 2

Simple strokes
a graceful dance across the walls and bridges
the Edgecliff angel
her mystery
and master unknown
repeated and repeated
an endless twirling
of tulle
lingering strokes
their tapering wispy ends
fringing this angel's gown
the painter's flow becomes a dance
becomes the dancer's flow
as she twists her circles
on walls, and gable ends
held up with obsessive fascination.

EC

Photo by Robert Montgomery

DIASPORIC DANNY

Danny Lim advocated for many causes during his time. More recently, Danny was attacked by a stranger and as a result was taken into a local intensive care unit (ICU).

Truth.
Arrested for
contentious
world views.
What sort of a character
raises money with
a four lettered word?
You care Danny,
an empathy for others' plight
never holding back,
turning heads,
hearts?
ICU.

EC

GLASGOW LEFT BEHIND

Music legend Jimmy Barnes left Glasgow with his family to start a new life in Australia in 1962. His works and his biographies share accounts of his experiences.

My heart is open, my mind's not closed
here in Sydney, the city where I've drifted South
to begin a new life, to settle down.
I wander in the city, part-tourist part-local,
along the walkway to MGA full of memories
when the lines of that Cold Chisel song
jangle across the esplanade
from the tourist crooner with didgeridoo.

These familiar words and tunes,
they make me think of past times,
of you Jimmy, of our old hometown Glasgow
and the diasporic life we both have.
Across the oceans we came,
different paths, different waves,
only other expats could understand
about the places, the people we left behind.

Australia 1962, how was this move for you?
Crossing oceans, time zones, dragging dreams
to settle down somewhere warm.
You sing of flame trees, of vets, of war.
I came so much later
my heart finding home here in Sydney
But I wonder, like you do I need to leave it once again
to know for sure...

EC

MARY MACKILLOP

Mary, Mary quite the lady
Aussie born with Scottish roots
crucifix on a string of beads
a desire to help always on show.

Let not the little given
nor even Australian abundance
hold us back as your motto declares
'Never leave a need unattended.'

Christian, a suffragette vision drove you,
Led to your divorce from your church.
Undeterred, you led by example,
we women shall not be ruled by men.

Now, at St Mary's Cathedral,
patriarchal landmark your statue stands
a monument to *'strength and gentleness.'*
activist for feminine employment
education for all, equality, justice.
Mary MacKillop, Australia's first saint.

EC

Photo by Elizabeth Cummings

SOCIAL PLACES: ANGEL AND MARTIN

Crucial communication points for more than 300 years.

Martin Place began resourcefully
as Sydney's water supplier.
Later, rose from locally quarried stone
now world-heritage listed.
Iconic structure former General Post Office,
today no longer for stamping mail
but a conduit for the social;
plush bars, definitive dining.

Angel Place on the other hand
artwork honouring the 50 species of birds
displaced after European settlement
gone but not forgotten
behold its beautiful recorded birdsong.

EC

CLOVER MOORE HAIKU

Over twenty years
Bligh member, incumbent Lord Mayor
first elected woman.

EC

HEARTBEAT CENTRE, SYDNEY CRICKET GROUND

Thump knock tap rhythm
pulsation pounding punching
throbbing drumming thudding.

Crowds, chants, claps.
Crazy cricket, balmy armies.
Wear your colours.
Chant your songs.
Hosts of stars
Don Bradman, Steve Waugh, Ricky Ponting,
Shane Warne, Allan Border,
A new era boasting feminine flair:
Ellye Perry, Beth Mooney, Alyssa Healy,
Meg Lanning, Ashleigh Gardner.
The names go on
The game goes on
The heartbeat never stops.

EC

Photo by Alessandro Bogliari

Photo by Anderson Mendes

Shining Places

Sydney Observatory

Warrane – Sydney Cove
highest point history told
first contact between the Eora
and the Berewalgal
this distant place people.
Established 1858
colonial structure
vantage point
for sea and stars
scopes searching
universes revealed
celestial wonders unfolding.
Aboriginal first stargazers
dreamings and stories
shared through generations
cosmic knowledge
eras of experience
makes one marvel
how science intersects
the capability
of traditional custodians.
Or can there be
a modern humility
for our naked eyes to see?
Open listening bringing wisdom
as the Dark Emu appears for all.

EC

Vivid

Ice-biting wind
greets me
as I turn the corner
night sky
its blackness beyond inky
scored with neon
splattered with a rainbow
sparkles across the harbour
where Luna Park lights up
a toytown whirling and spinning.
Imagine the squeals!
Then I turn to face the light show
a marvelous, groovy world
unfolding across buildings;
Customs House tonight baroque and terrifying
the Opera House sails a palette ablaze
The Rocks with iconic faces and places
a perennial winter delight.
Vividly, this is Sydney.

EC

Photo by Anderson Mendes

Vivid Sydney

Vivid an annual Sydney outdoor event at Circular Quay, The Rocks, Barangaroo, Martin Place, Darling Harbour, and Tumbalong Park.

So many Sydney icons
furnished and burnished with streams and beams
of light. Shafts extensive and rays relentless
vibrant and various! Vivid!
Flamboyant colours, blushing and rushing
and radiating immediate present and past,
signalling an ongoing 'presence' too.
Brilliant, glittery, luminous,
blazing and blinding,
fulgent and binding
Vibrant! Various! Vivid!

LH

Vivid Haiku

History ablaze
Across a youthful city
Lighting many hearts

LH

Photo by Anderson Mendes

Photo by Anderson Mendes

The Art Gallery of NSW

Drawing crowds
to know more
of the inner voice of a city,
of a people.
landscape secrets,
portraits gaze,
past stories live,
the times of artists,
evocations and insights
and foretellings
always holding our gaze,
leaving us closer and yet
leaving us wondering...

Impressive buildings lure us
into the atmosphere of art and artist
the wonder, the humour, artfulness, playfulness,
past and present colliding across tiled floors,
elevators lifting us to other cultures other times,
escalators helping us descend to changing exhibitions,
comforting chink of café life
telling us time to eat, drink, talk
and make those ineffable judgments,
leaving us closer and yet
leaving us wondering too...

LH

Stairs at Macquarie Street

After running the Sydney Marathon

Stairs. Stairs and more bloody stairs,
each step
requiring gladiator agility.
We lurch side to side
clutching race bags and energy drinks
our hopping staggering gait
testament to our efforts,
medals swinging, proud.
Satisfied until she bounds past us
and we read her T-shirt
100 marathons completed
in memory of my brother.
We applaud her loss and love
newly inspired.

EC

Photo by Dominic Kurniawan Suryaputra

State Library NSW – The Reading Room

The silence of intent
heads bowed; backs bent
this gentle lure of silence
church-like ambience
stained glass background.
The scholar draws upon
the calm the comfort of order
temporary safety from chaos
in reading's grace
within the arc of being doing yearning.

Student scholars passing by
the baleful glance at talkers,
the balm of solid books
on solid shelves floor to ceiling
arranged just so.
Book by book, rigid spines to tell.
Library on the edge of city's thrum,
the floors beneath the readers
a yawning heritage of archives.
Only the sound of breathing.
Peace here.

LH

Shakespeare in Sydney

State Library NSW 2023. After a visit to For All Time: Shakespeare in Print ***exhibition and the Shakespeare Room.***

Shakespeare in the Globe at play,
Shakespeare round the globe today,
in our speech unguarded knowing,
in our memory strung and glowing,
insights easy, ever flowing.
The slings and arrow of outrageous fortune.
Ambitious, powerful, frail and flawed
he tells our story with kiss, with sword,
at peace, in flight, small victories won,
where enchantments are yet undone.
We are such stuff as dreams are made on.
in language knotted and divine,
miracl'd his febrile mind.

Let last words here be his to say,
angel-tongue of word and play.
Not *cruel to be kind* or the clever *barefaced*,
not *be all and end all* or *wild goose chase*
not *into thin air* or *I know not 'seems'*
not *brave new world* or *midsummer night's dream.*
400 years strong, theatre and page,
timeless warning, *'All the world's a stage.'*

LH

Religious Reflection

Each and every pillar soars heavenwards
balanced in precise dignity
yet what mercy can be expected?
Are believers protected?
This is a place of beauty yet graphic horror
with its tableaux-decorated walls
upholding and bearing witness
to the Twelve Stations of the Cross.
Much stained glass,
the perfection of poise and balance,
art and architecture.

How do we even begin to understand
the process, the time, the belief
it took to build this cathedral?
It is this thought that has
my lips whispering,
'Oh my God!'

EC

Photo by Elizabeth Cummings

At the Cathedral

In the comforting gloom
Subsumed
A strange, stained peace resides.
Flashes of unholy history
Ebb away
And there's only today
Inside the towering gloom
And the incense
And the faint music
And the faint prayers
And the way out into the light,
To see another wedding group captured
On the joyous steps out there.

LH

State Theatre Foyer – A Memory

From verse novel Through a Glass Darkly

State Theatre glittering grand foyer,
He, the handsome new man in her life,
always stage-managed places for her,
being impecunious as he explained,
but not without imagination. Never!

Once it had been the grand chandelier-lit foyer,
the State Theatre with its sweeping double staircase,
its marble pillars and columns,
flamboyant with marble insets.
Marble, marble, its luxury spread everywhere,
white, green, brindle with the tile-studded floor,
and he welcomed her,
she the student who'd rushed from the bus
over eager, as if into his own place, a place perhaps
into his heart as he'd once dramatically declaimed.

The cloying theatre smell,
the burring words and intermittent music
from the famous Wurlitzer organ rising up from the stage
floating from that plush interior curtained place.
And just the two of them out here, foyered.

Purply padded chairs tempting with their golden arms,
a glittering velvety subdued place to hold hands,
his soft grey male-smelling coat,
his old leather briefcase slung on the seat,
his intimate words just for her.
Their place, content to sit in borrowed splendour
until actual time intervened, time to leave,
and they were disgorged out into real life,
the disquieting ordinariness of Sydney streets.

LH

Photo by John Toxteth

Sydney Museum

This is Bridge St
This Gadigal land
Something's happening here.
A plaque to tell us
first Government House
1788 to 1845 stone blocks reveal.
Something's happening here
29 towering poles
inscripted clan poles tell hard stories,
wood, steel and stone.
Look closer
human hair, feathers, ashes,
stories savage, startling, beautiful
markings, carvings, words,
a kind of fusion of the past and now.
Unsatisfactory collision
can lead to revelation.
This is Bridge St
This Gadigal land

LH

The Museum of Sydney

Place of change ironically
this museum on Bridge St
history both Aboriginal and Colonial.
How might we represent
the wealth and wonder of this land?
Wooden lottery balls of luck and chance,
surrounding buildings juxtaposing old and new,
architectural designs, diaphanous light-bearing
underscore requisite shrewd symbols
of a new culture,
one that holds the shameful history
with a head held high for the future,
righting of wrongs.
Totems to a fresh understanding
affirming that this *is* Gadigal land.

EC

Photo by Libby Hathorn

Photo by Anderson Mendes

Hymn to Diamond City Sydney

Shimmer glow harbour nights
glitter days of harbour lights
sapphire studded, emerald green
slivers of silver in between.

Diamond city Sydney
slow, slow and fast paced
shining city Sydney
metropolis blue-water graced.

Shimmer glow harbour nights
glitter days of harbour lights
Sydney a city to know and to sing
absorbing all the charms it brings.

LH

Photo by Elizabeth Cummings

This is the spell of the Grand Old Harbour

This is the spell of the harbour green,
With sapphire blue moments, currents keen,
Sunlight dancing in diamonds serene.

This is the spell of the harbour blue
Reclaimed foreshore Barangaroo
(Did she pass by this swerving rock
Aboriginal woman to fish at this spot?)

This is the spell of the harbour bright
The thrum of a city day and night
Sydney, Sydney city of grace,
a shining welcoming open face...

LH

Authors

Libby Hathorn

Translated into several languages and adapted for stage and screen, Libby's work has won honours in Australia, United States, Great Britain and the Netherlands. She is the recipient of several literary awards and two of her works have become operas for which she wrote the libretti. She lives and works in Sydney.

www.libbyhathorn.com

Agent Fiona Inglis at Curtis Brown, Sydney
www.curtisbrown.com.au/contact

Elizabeth Cummings

Elizabeth Cummings. An experienced presenter and guest lecturer in mental health and creative writing both locally and internationally. Her collaborative creative projects include adapting her stories into puppet performances by the Lithuanian State Puppet Theatre. Sydney-based Elizabeth has previously won the South Coast Writers Prize for her poetry.

elizabethmarycummings.com

Acknowledgements

Elizabeth Cummings

- *Standing in Waverley Cemetery*. First published *Coastal Poetry*, 2023.
- *Sydney's Coastal Surprise: Bondi to Coogee Walk*. First published *Coastal Poetry*, 2023.
- *Connecting Souls*. Inspired by song *Khe Sanh* by Jimmy Barnes, 1978.
- *Vivid*. First published in *Women's Ink* SWW NSW, 2025.
- *Sydney Observatory*. First published in *Women's Ink* SWW NSW, 2025.

Libby Hathorn

- *Bondi Beach Supreme.* First published *Coastal Poetry*, 2023.
- *Two Bondi Beach haiku.* First published *Coastal Poetry*, 2023.
- *I Love the Trams.* First published Dept of Education, *S* Magazine, 2022
- State Theatre extract from verse novel *Through a Glass Darkly*, 2026
- *Shakespeare First Folio* lines from *Macbeth, Hamlet*, by William Shakespeare
- *This is the Spell of the Grand old Harbour* influenced by the poem *Spells* by James Reeve
- *The Rocks*. First published in *Women's Ink* SWW NSW, 2025.

Shining City Sydney, first edition
Published by Pacific Ocean Press, 2025
Designed by Rosie Handley
Printed by Pegasus Print Sydney
Type is set in Barlow
ISBN 978-1-922451-14-9

Cover images by Anderson Mendes
Principal photographer Anderson Mendes
@andersonmendes